JUNGLE CRASH!

Sarah Levete

Published 2011 by
A&C Black Publishers Ltd.
36 Soho Square, London, W1D 3QY

www.acblack.com

ISBN HB 978-1-4081-3381-1
      PB 978-1-4081-3380-4

Every effort has been made to trace copyright holders and to obtain their permission for use of copyright material. The author and publishers would be pleased to rectify any error or omission in future editions.

This book is produced using paper that is made from wood grown in managed, sustainable forests. It is natural, renewable and recyclable. The logging and manufacturing processes conform to the environmental regulations of the country of origin.

Produced for A&C Black by Calcium. www.calciumcreative.co.uk

Printed and bound in China by C&C Offset Printing Co.

All the internet addresses given in this book were correct at the time of going to press. The author and publishers regret any inconvenience caused if addresses have changed or sites have ceased to exist, but can accept no responsibility for any such changes.

Acknowledgements

The publishers would like to thank the following for their kind permission to reproduce their photographs:

Cover: Shutterstock
Pages: Dreamstime: Maurie Hill 21, Mtphotostock 11, Nael Pictures 18, Roman Shiyanov 16; Photolibrary: Stock Byte 8; Shutterstock: Bayberry 10, Alexander Chaikin 4, Fouquin 20, Joe Gough 5, Guentermanaus 17, Jklingebiel 6, Stephen Mcsweeny 3, 9, Photoinnovation 19, Dr. Morley Read 13, Jamie Robinson 1, 15, SNEHIT 7, Szefei 14, Worldswildlifewonders 12.

Contents

Jungle of Trees

In the **jungle**, a thick carpet of trees and plants covers the ground. Lots of tiny **insects** and large animals live in the jungle.

Jungle crash!

Many trees are being chopped down in jungles around the world. Find out what happens to animals and plants when a tree in the jungle crashes to the ground.

Animals such as this lizard live in jungle trees.

Gone in minutes

It takes years for a tree to grow but it only takes minutes to cut it down.

Wood Wanted

Wood comes from trees. People cut down trees for the wood. They also cut down trees in the jungle so they can grow food there.

Animal home

Orangutans live in jungles in Asia, high up in the trees. But lots of their trees have been chopped down and cut up for wood. The wood from the trees is used all over the world.

Without trees, orangutans have nowhere to live.

Made of wood

Wood that has been cut from trees is called timber. It is used to make many things including paper and furniture.

For the Chop

People who cut down trees are called **loggers**. They use machines to cut down the trees and to clear space for roads.

Big machines

Jungles are far from roads and towns, so loggers build roads to reach them. They use large machines such as **bulldozers**, trucks, and diggers to make new roads in the jungle.

Bulldozer

 Big machines clear the ground.

Deadly

Big machines smash up plants and small trees – along with the insects and animals that live in them.

Watch Out

A noisy **chainsaw** slices through a thick tree trunk in minutes. The tree topples over, crashing into other trees and plants.

Taken out

The tree is then taken away to be cut up into pieces. Sometimes loggers use chainsaws to chop up the tree in the jungle. Then the wood is sold to people around the world.

 Powerful chainsaws cut through lots of wood quickly.

Chainsaw

Taken away

When the wood has been cut into pieces, it is loaded onto a lorry and sent to other countries.

11

No Homes

Back in the jungle, the trees that animals once lived in have gone. Now all of these animals no longer have a home.

Huge harpy

In Central and South America, many of the jungle trees that **harpy eagles** live in have been cut down for their wood. With their homes **destroyed**, few harpy eagles now live in the wild.

 Harpy eagles live high up in the trees.

We all live here

Many insects live on one tree, so if the tree is cut down they all lose their home.

Nothing to Eat

Many birds eat fruit that grows on jungle trees. But if the fruit trees are cut down, these birds have nothing to eat and will die.

No new trees

When birds eat fruit, they drop **seeds** that will grow into trees. With no fruit to eat, the birds will not drop seeds. This means no new fruit trees will grow in the jungle.

 Great hornbill birds love tasty fruit.

We need fruit

Spider monkeys also eat fruit that grows on fruit trees in Central and South American jungles. If the trees are cut down they will have nothing to eat.

Jungle People

People also live in jungles, so when jungle trees are cut down, the homes of jungle people are destroyed too.

Jungle home

Some people have lived in jungles for many years. They know how to **survive** there without harming the jungle.

 Jungle people share the forest with the animals, trees, and plants.

More trouble

People from cities are moving to the jungle. Many trees are cut down to make room for them.

Healthy Trees

Wood is important, but so are trees! Trees help to keep the air healthy and they give us food to eat and important **medicines**.

Jungle medicine

Lots of the medicines we use come from plants and trees that grow in the jungle. **Botanists** are discovering more amazing jungle plants and trees every day.

Save the trees

We need to save jungle trees because everything in the jungle suffers when too many trees are cut down for wood.

Scientists use amazing jungle plants to create powerful medicines.

Chopped Safely

Every time a tree is chopped down, a jungle animal loses its home. There are things everyone can do to help **protect** them.

Stop cutting, start growing

People can stop cutting down so many jungle trees. New trees can also be planted so that jungle animals have somewhere to live, but it would take a *lot* of trees to replace trees that have been cut down. If people look after the trees, then jungle animals will always have homes.

Tree frogs need trees!

Safe to grow

People can grow trees in special areas called **reserves**. Loggers are not allowed to chop down trees here.

Glossary

botanists people who study trees and plants

bulldozers large vehicles with a big shovel

chainsaw tool with a large saw

destroyed ruined

harpy eagles large birds that hunt animals for food

insects creatures with six legs

jungle hot place with many trees

loggers people who cut down trees

medicines things that make people better if they are ill

orangutans apes with long, red, and shaggy hair

protect keep safe

reserves places in which trees and wildlife are protected

seeds parts of a plant from which new plants grow

spider monkeys monkeys that have long tails. They use their tails to grip on to branches as they climb.

survive to be able to stay alive

Further Reading

Websites

Find out lots more about rainforests and the animals that live there at:
www.enchantedlearning.com/subjects/rainforest

Discover more about rainforests, the animals and plants that live there, and why rainforests have so much rain at:
www.globio.org/glossopedia/article.aspx?art_id=6

Books

Rainforest (Eye Wonder) by Elinor Greenwood, Dorling Kindersley (2001).

Rainforest (Usborne Beginners) by Lucy Beckett-Bowman, Usborne (2008).

Rainforests (Totally Weird) by Kate Graham, Two-Can (1998).

Index